I-SPY

with David Bellamy

GARDEN BIRDS

I-Spy Books
12 Star Road, Partridge Green
Horsham, Sussex RH13 8RA

GARDEN BIRDS

Imagine a garden without birds! Well, I'd rather not and fortunately for us all gardens, however small, or wherever they are located, are visited by birds. To see some sorts, though, we may need to go into other gardens, like public parks with big trees and perhaps a lake. And we are very lucky in Britain because there are many stately and other homes which are famous for their gardens.

What is more, many of them, thanks both to their owners and the National Trust, are open to the public at various times of the year, and most of them are ideal bird gardens.

So hang on to your pencils and your Garden Bird Book . . . here we go, and remember—many of these birds will visit your own garden if only you make them welcome!

SCORING

As you spot each of the birds here—and answer the simple question—you can earn an I-SPY score. When your scores total 1250 you may award yourself the rank of BIRD OBSERVER with Silver Honours. When they reach a complete total of 1500 points you are entitled to the rank of BIRD OBSERVER with Gold Honours; you may then send your book to me, and I shall return it to you stamped with my personal seal. Your certificate of rank is on the inside-back-cover of this book.

Good hunting!

YOUR OWN BIRD TABLE

One easy way of studying birds is to attract them to your garden by putting a bird table there. Bird tables can be almost any size and shape; all you need is a flat platform about 30cm × 45cm (12″ × 18″) of exterior quality, or marine, plywood fixed on a post or hanging from a tree.

To keep food on the table and to allow water to drain off, screw on wooden sides leaving gaps at each corner. A roof is not necessary.

Practically all kitchen scraps are acceptable— bread (preferably brown), stale cake, potatoes, chopped bacon rind, fat, cheese, meat bones, apple cores, etc. Shelled peanuts (*not* salted) are great favourites with the tit family, or unshelled, hung on a string. Suet is good for cold weather and so is a coconut (*not* dessicated) cut into two halves. Remember, also, to put out water as well as food.

You may care to join The YOUNG ORNITHOLOGISTS' CLUB, so look on page 46.

Score **50** *for putting up a bird table in your garden.*

We'll start scoring with a species that can be found really nearly everywhere, and work along to those that will take a bit of Spying.

HOUSE SPARROW

Take people away from Britain and in time the ever so common House Sparrow would probably become extinct. This tiny bird lives with and depends on man. It is not territorial and, in fact, lives in loose nesting colonies grouped together in, say, one part of a housing estate. House Sparrows remain faithful to their mates until death do them part. What is more, they return to the same nest year after year.

I-SPY a House Sparrow .... Score **10**

I-SPY the nest colony area .... Score **20**

What colour are young sparrow legs? .... Score **20**

The most abundant wild bird is the African Red-billed Quelea, a sort of sparrow, probably about 10,000,000,000 of them in all!

STARLING

A very common and beautiful bird. See its iridescent feathers, green through purple, depending on how the sun catches them. They are very sociable birds and fly and roost in flocks. They even visit gardens in small groups, strutting about together as if they owned the place.

I-SPY a Starling .... Score **10**

I-SPY a Starling roost in town .... Score **25**

50,000 Starlings in one roost site is not unusual. 1,000,000,000 Starlings in the world, that's an awful lot of feathers to be preened.

TOWN PIGEON

You know, the ones that live in Trafalgar Square and in most towns. Descendants of the white rumped Rock Dove, they have come to take up residence on the cliff-like buildings of our towns and, coo, they don't half make a mess! Despite their enormous colour variation, many still retain the white rump of their ancestors.

I-SPY a Town Pigeon—careful, there are other sorts (see page 13) .... Score **10**

BLACKBIRD

A common sight in most gardens. The male is glossy black with brilliant yellowish-orange bill and eye rims. I-SPY a raised, slightly spread tail, and—when he is on the ground—downward sloping wings. The female is brown—dark above, and rather reddish below. She has a whitish chin and a brown bill (occasionally I-SPY blackbirds with patches of white; or even a complete albino).

Blackbirds start courting at about Christmas, and they start to defend their territories from late February to early March. Listen to them sing from the top of a tree, or even a TV aerial.

I-SPY the male defending its territory..................Score **15**

I-SPY Blackbirds eating fruit..................................Score **10**

I-SPY Blackbirds eating insects or worms...✔...Score **10**

ROBIN

A plump little bird with rich orange-red colouring on breast and forehead. In contrast, the rest of the body is a quiet olive-brown.

The most territorial of all our birds. He owns your garden and he knows it. Both cock and hen are especially aggressive and will even fight to keep other birds out of the area.

I-SPYed a Robin at .... Score **10**

I-SPY aggressive behaviour .... Score **20**
I-SPY a nest site (don't go near between February and

July) .... Score **25**

DUNNOCK OR HEDGE SPARROW

Not really a sparrow at all, but one of the Accentors, small birds which search about on the ground for insects and spiders to eat, turning to seeds mainly in the cold of winter. They are like female House Sparrows, but—

*I-SPY a narrow bill (ideal for catching insects)*Score **10**

I-SPY a dark grey head and underside......................Score **5**

Most birds build nests, so do many fish, including sticklebacks.

WREN

I-SPY brown plumage with bars of darker colouring, and a stumpy uptilted tail. Male Wrens begin building nests in February, not waiting for spring or a mate.

I often see them rushing about in my flower beds looking for insects among the leaf litter. One good reason for being an untidy gardener!

Listen for its rich song—seems far too loud for such a tiny bird..Score **15**

BLUE TIT

The only tit with this brilliant blue colouring on wings, tail and crown. Under-parts are primrose yellow, the back is greenish, the cheeks white, and there is a black line running across the eye.

I reckon that this is everyone's favourite garden bird, even if it does peck through the milk bottle caps.

I-SPY a Blue Tit..Score **10**

GREAT TIT

The largest of the tits. He's a great "show-off" and will perform all kinds of acrobatic tricks.

I-SPY a yellow breast with a black central stripe......................
Score **10**

COAL TIT

MARSH TIT

COAL TIT

A small, cobby bird.

I-SPY a white patch on the back of its neck ....Score **25**

MARSH TIT

I-SPY what looks like a Coal Tit, but without a white patch on the back of its head ....Score **25**

LONG-TAILED TIT

Often seen in winter groups flitting along hedgerows.

I-SPY a very small black and white body with a long, long tail ....Score **20**

Birds lay eggs, so do fish.
Two more pigeons, but really wild ones this time.

WOOD PIGEON

A much larger bird than the Town Pigeon, from which it can be readily distinguished by the white bar on the top of each wing. A real pest to farmers but a very beautiful bird to see in the garden. Wood Pigeons are on the increase.

I-SPY a Wood Pigeon ....Score **10**

I-SPY its stick platform nest. They nest in conifers in my garden. How about the whitebeams in your road? Take a look. ....Score **30**

COLLARED DOVE　　　　　　　　　　　**WOOD PIGEON**

COLLARED DOVE

It only arrived in Britain in 1955 and is now common throughout the British Isles. A native of India, but in the last 70 years has made itself at home across Europe. Nice to see, with its grey brown plumage, black wing tips and striking black collar, but like the other pigeons it is often an unwelcome visitor both to the gardener and farmer alike. And its monotonous call-notes can be a bit irritating!

I-SPY the black collar ....Score **25**

I-SPY pigeons courting ....Score **35**

Some birds defend their territories, so do many fish. I remember being chased away by a tiny trigger fish who didn't like me diving near his nest.

Where did all the birds originally come from? What prehistoric animals developed into birds?—Read all about it in I-Spy Dinosaurs. *'Can one spy dinosaurs?' I hear you ask. Well, look at the book and find out!*

Now for some
FINCHES

Here is a group of birds, all of which live in open woodlands, or the margins of woods and forests. So when man came along and made fields and, more recently, gardens, they all came to enjoy everything a well kept garden estate has to offer. They are small birds with stout, short beaks designed for cracking open tough seeds.

Remember, it was the sorts of finches living on the Galapagos Islands which helped Charles Darwin to realise the role of natural selection in nature. He had a super garden around his house at Downe in Kent and I bet all our finches visited him there.

Chaffinch
Britain's commonest bird, and through binoculars certainly one of our most colourful. The ones in my garden enjoy the patch of weeds with Plantains, Docks, Shepherds Purse and the edge of the lawn, which I leave unmown to set seed. This is also our only territorial finch, who will guard his chosen area against all comers.

I-SPY a Chaffinch...Score **10**
I-SPY a white shoulder patch, wing bar and cleft tail......
Score **10**

Male Chaffinches say 'Pink, pink', and what is more the male has pink feathers on its tum.

Greenfinch

Likes to nest in shrubs, eats insects early in the year and weed seeds during the summer. Will visit a bird table for peanuts and is quite an acrobat, but is very aggressive and may well chase the other birds off. Yellow patches on the wing and sides of the tail. Sociable while breeding and several may nest in the same bush.

I-SPY their flesh pink legs..................................Score **10**
I-SPY their bounding flight.................................Score **10**
Listen for the buzzing song...............................Score **10**

Some birds fly in flocks, some fish swim in shoals. This way they gain protection from their enemies.

Two beautiful finch species. And listen for their very different songs.

Goldfinch

Most typically you will see these birds swaying precariously on the flowering stems of Thistles, Burdock and Teasels, feasting on the seeds. Like the Greenfinches, they are not particularly territorial — perhaps because they feed on seeds which are plentiful during the time they are feeding their young. Plumage is a striking mixture of red, white, black, yellow and brown. Nest mainly in trees.

I-SPY a Goldfinch..Score **20**
I-SPY the pale pink bill..Score **5**

Bullfinch

Not a welcome visitor to a vegetable garden. They have a softer bill than the other finches and cannot, therefore, crack open the hard seeds and so go for soft, juicy buds in a big way. The male is really magnificent with bright pink cheeks and underparts, with a white rump and wing bars.

I-SPY a Bullfinch ....Score **25**

What colour was his bill?..Score **10**

Some birds migrate. The Eel, a fish which is still common in many British rivers, travels 6,500 kms to its breeding grounds in the Sargasso Sea on the other side of the Atlantic.

THE THRUSHES

If you see a bird with a speckled breast pulling a worm out of your lawn, it's a thrush, and very beautiful they are too. Their songs are just as beautiful.

Two resident species:

Song Thrush
I-SPY a Thrush with no white tips to its tail feathers..Score **10**
I hear his song, in which each note is repeated twice...Score **10**
I-SPY a stone surrounded by broken snail shells...Score **25**
This is called an anvil and it is the feeding place of a Song Thrush.

Mistle Thrush
Slightly larger than a Song Thrush, and tends to keep its distance. Look for it singing high in a tree.

I-SPY a well spotted breast..Score **10**
I-SPY white tips to the tail and a grey brown back...........
Score **10**

Many birds perform ritual displays (even on my lawn). Many fish, including the Giant Manta Ray, do the same, though not in my garden.

Two Winter-visiting thrushes that nest in the north and come south for our milder winters. Often seen in parks.

Fieldfare
Look for them on winter playing fields or in hawthorn hedges eating berries, and listen for their 'chack chack' flight call.

I-SPY a blue-grey head and rump......................... Score **25**

Redwing The smallest common thrush. In appearance it's rather like the Song Thrush, but I-SPY a broad creamy eye-stripe, chestnut-red flanks, and a streaked—not spotted—breast. During winter you may see large flocks feeding in open pasture and grasslands, and very likely you'll see Redwings and Fieldfares together.

What date did you see yours? .... Score **25**

Birds call to each other, so do many fish, although it is much more difficult underwater to identify the fish with the noise, but we are learning all the time.

Now, what about some warm weather birds— summer visitors.

SWALLOW

SWALLOW

Swallow swoops, skims, wheels in flight. A graceful bird.

Watch for the long streamers from the forked tail and for the metallic blue sheen of the back, wings and tail. The forehead and the upper parts of the throat are chestnut-red; the underparts are a creamy white. A lover of farmland and open country, but watch for it over park lakes.

I-SPY a Swallow .... Score **20**

HOUSE MARTIN

Builds colonies of distinctive nests of mud under the eaves of houses. If they do decide to come and share your house, they can make quite a mess. However, my advice is enjoy it.

I-SPY a short-tailed blue-black bird with a white rump and underparts..Score **20**

HOUSE MARTIN

SWIFT

SWIFT

Not really in the same group of birds as the Swallows and Martins. It is their weird cries which give them their other names, Devil Bird, Devil's Screamer and many more. These birds actually go to sleep while on the wing, in fact they only come to rest on a solid object when they are nesting. They nest in roofs, even in the centre of the busiest cities. You can make them specially welcome by having a nest box rather than a window box (see page 45).

I-SPY their curved scimitar-shaped wings........Score **15**
I hear their screaming call..................................Score **15**

WOODPECKERS

Birds which are usually heard long before they are seen and, yes, they do visit gardens, even in towns.

GREEN WOODPECKER   GREAT SPOTTED WOODPECKER

Green Woodpecker
Our only green bird with red on its head, also known as the Yaffle or Rain Bird. Often seen on lawns, probing for ants.

I-SPY its yellow rump..Score **25**

Ask Granny or Grandad what they called it.

Great Spotted Woodpecker
Also known by the much more apt name of Pied Woodpecker. A large bird with a prominent white wing patch. This one causes a great stir when he or she visits my bird table.

I-SPY the way it uses its tail as a prop while climbing a tree..Score **25**

NUTHATCH

Another tree climber, and this one can climb both up and down the trunk. Mainly found in the southern half of Britain, it will visit bags of peanuts hung up by the window. It will also take nuts with hard shells, jam them into crevices in the bark and hammer them open with its strong beak.

I-SPY a Nuthatch..Score **25**
I hang peanuts out for the birds...........................Score **20**

NUTHATCH

TREE CREEPER

TREE CREEPER

Here's a bird which enjoys a garden with lots of trees, and the bigger the better—it loves ivy.

A curved beak, white belly and the way it scuttles up the tree in a spiral searching out the insects in the bark gives it away. At first sight you might think that it is a mouse, not a bird.

What does it do with its tail as it climbs the bark?............

....

Does it climb back down the tree?.....................Score **25**

The longest feather I have ever found in my garden was 42cm (16½"). It belonged to a pheasant.

WARBLERS

Small birds which flit through the garden in an incessant search for insects to eat. Their warbling song often gives them away before you can see them. Summer visitors except for the

Blackcap

If you see one in winter, it's been nesting in Scandinavia and has moved south. Our summer visitors go to Spain and North Africa for the winter.

A short warble and a black-capped male and brown-capped female aid identification. A bird that likes Rhododendrons in which to hide and sing.

I-SPY a Blackcap..Score **25**

Garden Warbler

A longer warble than the Blackcap and a uniform pale brown colour with no distinctive markings, just slightly paler beneath, make this a difficult one. Though bearing the name Garden, they are rarely found in small ones.

I-SPY a uniform brown bird which belongs to that warbling song..Score **25**

Chiffchaff and Willow Warbler

Two small, dainty summer visitors easily mistaken for one another. You'll recognise the Chiffchaff *(left)* the moment you hear his song: 'chiff-chiff' or 'chiff-chaff'. The Willow Warbler has a quiet, sweet song.

Both birds are olive above, and whitish-buff with just a trace of lemon below. There's one difference, however. The legs of the Chiffchaff are almost black; those of the Willow Warbler are lightish brown.

Score for seeing either of them, passing through your garden or along a hedgerow..**15**

Last year the first Cuckoo cuckooed in my garden on 24th April. The earliest British record is for Oxfordshire—2nd March 1972. Easier heard than seen, so no score—just enjoy the sound!

SPOTTED FLYCATCHER

Nests on buildings and tree trunks. You will see them sitting on a perch and making short darting flights to catch an insect. Listen, you can actually hear its beak snap shut! If you don't disturb them they will return to the same perch time and time again.

I-SPY its upright pose while waiting on a perch.............
Score **25**
I-SPY spotted birds, but only when they are young— the adults are streaky breasted........................Score **30**

PIED WAGTAIL

A bird which enjoys a large lawn. Watch its long tail bobbing up and down as it runs about in search of insects. If you have a garden pond, then the insects from that will also help feed it. Often assembles in huge roosts in towns in winter.

I-SPY this dapper black and white bird.................Score **10**
   and its dainty walk and bobbing tail................Score **5**

THE CROW FAMILY

Have you ever tried perching on a branch?

If you do try, then please choose one only a few centimetres above the ground because you will find it very difficult. Now imagine that the branch is swaying about in a force 9 gale. What a way to try and rest, let alone go to sleep! Well, all perching birds do it with ease for the simple reason that when they perch the weight of their bodies acts on a special system of muscles and tendons which make their claws grip on the perch.

The Crow family includes the largest of our perching birds, the Raven. Next biggest is:

Carrion Crow

Carrion Crow because they eat carrion, the dead remains of other birds and animals, thus helping to keep the countryside clean and healthy. Often rests in town parks.

I-SPY a big black bird—or 2....................................Score **10**

If there are lots and are in the country, they'll probably
be:

Rooks
'Caw caw' is their raucous call and I tell you when the
200 which live in the rookery at the bottom of my
garden all take off on a spring morning, it's much
more efficient than an alarm clock. They are big birds
46cm (check it on a ruler) long.

*I-SPY big black birds with a grey spot at the base of
their beaks*...Score **15**

Jackdaw
Much more likely to be seen in a village garden, but I
have seen them in towns. They have a black body, but
the back of their head and neck is a most wonderful
grey.

I-SPY a Jackdaw's jerky walk.................................Score **15**

Magpie
Its black and white body with a very long tail makes it
almost unmistakable, and, even when in flight, its
long glides and rapid flaps give the game away.

*I-SPY two Magpies (it's said to be luckier than seeing
one)*..Score **15**

Jay
Get a close look at this one and you might even think
you were in the tropics. So bright are their colours,
especially the blue wing patch. Raucous calling is the
first sign that you have one about. Like Magpies, they
often visit gardens, even in towns.

I-SPY a Jay...Score **15**

The rarest bird I have ever spied is the Mauritian Kestrel—there are only about 23 left.

KESTREL

If you see a bird of prey hovering over your garden—yes, even in the centre of London—it is probably a Kestrel. Constant hovering with vigorous wing flapping is by far and away the best characteristic.

I-SPY a hovering Kestrel...Score **15**
I-SPY it pounce on to its prey...........................Score **30**

KESTREL▲   ▼ SPARROWHAWK

SPARROWHAWK

Another bird of prey to watch for, quite often round towns and villages. I-SPY its short wings and dashing flight along hedgerows looking for small birds.

TAWNY OWL

OWLS

The only other large predator which may be seen, or more often heard, around town gardens is the Tawny Owl.

I hear his 'Ke-wick ke-wick' call and wavering hoot............
Score **10**
I see him swoop silently across the garden......Score **20**

NOW FOR SOME BIG BIRDS

I've got a pet swan in my garden. She is called Wellington (We gave her her name before we found out what sex she was). She came to live with us after losing a wing and has been a great friend of the family ever since. Now, you probably won't have a swan in your garden, so let's cheat a bit—how about some birdwatching in a public garden, your local park.

MUTE SWAN

I-SPY a bright orange bill.
I-SPY the large black knob at the base of the bill.
Wellington is a Mute Swan—swans are large ducks.
I-SPY them tail up in the water..................................Score **10**
Swans are vegetarian.

Whooper Swans flew over my garden two years ago, and they hold the bird world altitude record of 8,230 metres.

CANADA GOOSE

Geese are intermediate in size between ducks and swans. This one was introduced from, where else but, Canada to live in our ponds and lakes.

I-SPY the long black neck and head, white throat and light breast..Score **15**
I-SPY Canada Goose goslings .... Score **20**
I-SPY Swan cygnets .... Score **20**

The young of all members of the duck tribe hatch with feathers already on and can swim almost at once. Never go near the nests of these or, indeed, any other birds on purpose. But, of course, you never would because you are members of the I-SPY CLUB and know all about these things.

DUCKS ON THE POND

It may be easy to recognise a duck, with its shovel-like beak and webbed feet which give it an awkward waddling gait on dry land, but what about the different types of duck and other water birds? Even quite a small lake in a town park may provide home for quite a variety.

Tufted Duck

The drakes are usually unmistakable with their white flanks, belly and wing bar all in marked contrast to their black bodies. A very dapper little diving duck, whose head is topped by a black crest. The females and juveniles are much more difficult to identify, as is the case with most sorts of duck. To begin with, the best thing to do is identify the males and then study the ones who are tagging along.

I-SPY Tufted Ducks diving for their dinner .... Score **15**

How long do they stay down? ....

Pochard

Another smart diving duck, with its numbers added to in winter by continental visitors .... Score **15**

Mallard

I-SPY the drake's dark green head......................Score **5**
I-SPY the ducks' and drakes' blue wing patch or speculum..Score **10**

Mallards are dabbling ducks, also known as surface feeders, which up-end to feed on plants underwater. They also jump out of the water when they take off to fly.

I-SPY the jump take-off of a dabbling duck..........Score **5**
I-SPY a diving duck running for lift-off...................Score **5**

Mandarin Duck

I-SPY the drake's orange side whiskers and orange wing fins...Score **15**
I-SPY the female's white eye ring, eye stripe and chin..Score **15**

A very handsome introduction from E. Asia, now wild in parks.

Before we leave the ducks and their kins, I must tell you all about the Wildfowl Trust, of which I am a member. It was founded by Sir Peter Scott, who is the son of a very famous explorer, and is himself an accomplished artist and a glider pilot. Its aim is to save wildfowl and waterfowl all over the world. They have very special wildfowl parks and refuges dotted all round the country. You can visit them and see waterfowl from all over the world; you can even adopt a duck while you are there. I'll give you the address later.

Two waterbirds, but not ducks—look at their feet, with unwebbed toes; and differently shaped beaks.

Moorhen
I-SPY its black body, red bill and shield............Score **10**
I-SPY its bobbing head as it swims and white tail...........
Score **5**

Coot
A bigger bird, often in groups.

I-SPY its black body, white bill and shield.........Score **10**
I-SPY it diving for its food...........Score **5**

How long did it stay under water?...........

SEAGULLS

They may be called gulls of the sea, but in recent years some of them have begun to move inland and take over our local rubbish dumps, scavenging rather than fishing for their food.

Lesser Black-backed Gull
I-SPY dark grey back and wings...........Score **20**
I-SPY yellow or orange legs (which)?...........Score **5**

a Black-Headed Gull

I-SPY its black head, but only in summer............ Score **10**
I-SPY the white edge on the front of its wing...... Score **5**

If the females are Sea Gulls, are the males Sea Buoys?

b Common Gull

This one is like the Herring Gull, but has a greenish yellow bill, without a red spot, and yellow green legs.

I-SPY a Common Gull.. Score **15**

c Herring Gull

I-SPY pale grey back and wings, and black and white wing tips.. Score **15**
I-SPY a red spot on a yellow bill............................ Score **5**
I-SPY pink legs... Score **5**

Now back from our flights of fancy around the pond in the park and the local rubbish tip, to the garden proper, for some less commonly seen small birds.

SISKIN

Another member of the finch family and a bird which is following the spread of conifer plantations south. A Birch tree may well attract them to your garden, but so will weed seeds too. They may even nest there if you have a conifer growing.

I-SPY the yellow colour of the male............................Score **15**

I-SPY the male's black chin and crown................Score **5**

REDPOLL

Another tiny finch, that likes conifers, Alder and Birch trees. Teams up with Siskins in winter.

I-SPY its red 'poll' and black chin............................Score **25**

TREE SPARROW

A sparrow in an old orchard or wood, that somehow doesn't look quite right, might be a Tree Sparrow. Look for a rich brown crown and dark cheek patches. Male and female are alike.

Where did you see yours? .... Score **25**

REED BUNTING

Used to live where its name says it should—in reedy edges of water and marsh, but is gradually changing to drier places, and in winter even turns up on the bird table—even in the middle of London!

Score for seeing one anywhere **20**

There are 8,600 different sorts of bird living in the world today. How many visit your garden?

BIRD GARDENING

You can do two things to make your garden attractive to birds. Give them food (and water)—both on a bird table (see p.3) and by planting food plants like berried shrubs and keeping some weeds in a wild corner; and give them nest sites—either in trees and shrubs or in boxes.

CATS AND GARDEN BIRDS

Even the best behaved cats like birds. It is built into their nature to hunt and however well fed some will always chase the birds in the garden. So a good addition to any bird garden is a shrub and/or a tree or two.

For a small garden the best shrubs and trees are the ones which provide the birds with most shelter, nest sites and food.

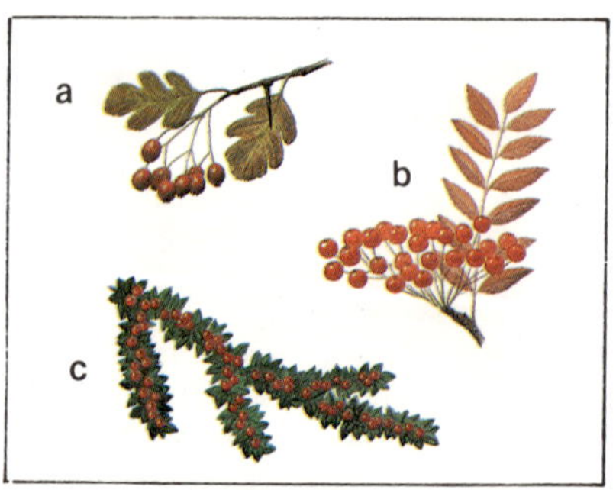

a   **HAWTHORN TREES**

With rose hips on the garden wall and a Hawthorn as a hedge, or standard tree, producing thousands of scarlet fruits called haws, your bird garden is really ready for visitors and resident birds alike. Also, super thorns will protect nesting birds from the wildest of cats.

b   **ROWAN TREES**

They grow quickly and not too big for the garden (take advice at the garden centre). Their smooth bark is not the easiest thing for a cat to climb and their branches are good for nest sites. Add to this the great saucers of insect-attracting flowers and masses of scarlet or orange fruits, and you have the perfect bird garden tree.

Lovely autumn colour from the leaves for us to enjoy, too!

c   **COTONEASTER**

You can either say COE TONE EE ASTER, or COTON EASTER, but however you say it, the birds love these shrubs, some of which can be trained to scramble up a wall or over a trellis or fence. They provide cover and a superabundance of orange or red berries *(again, good for birds but not for us humans)* in the autumn and winter.

CLIMBING ROSES

These are good, both for the people and the birds. For us they provide flowers in abundance, and for the birds a nest site protected by all the spines and prickles, an abundance of insect visitors for food in the summer, and gorgeous red rose hips for food in the autumn and winter.

BARBERRY

Barberry bushes, and there are a lot to choose from, are very spiny things and so provide protection. They also provide an abundance of flowers which attract insects—food for the birds—and, if the insects do their job properly, lots of juicy fruit. When the Barberry is in flower you might like to try an experiment. Take a very fine twig or straw and gently touch the anthers of the flowers. You will see that they flick inwards very violently, covering the tip of the twig with pollen. Try again . . . moving plants right in your (sorry, the robin's) own back yard.

N.B. No scoring for vegetation, but turn to page 46.

"Forty fousand feavers on a frush . . . " that's how the song goes. The record is 25,216 feathers on a Whistling Swan.

Now for nest boxes. They're easy to make and aren't meant to last for years, so don't creosote or paint them—or when the summer sun gets on them you'll stink the poor birds out!

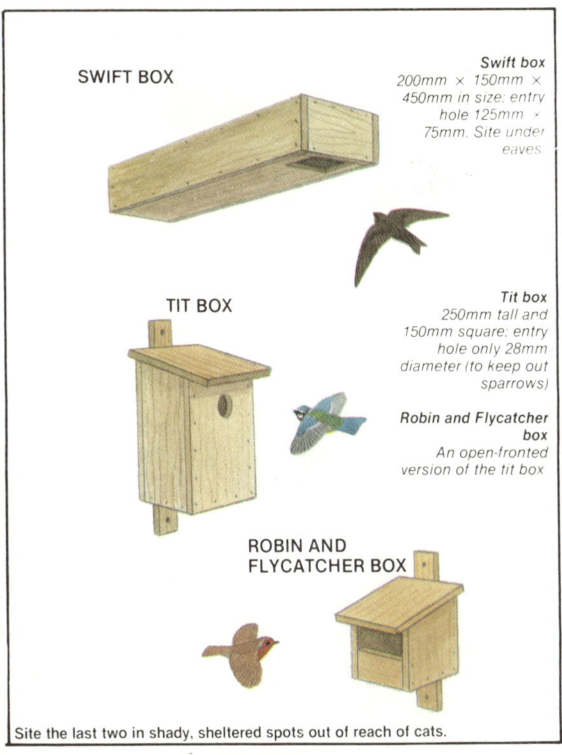

Now if you are really interested, join the Young Ornithologists' Club, learn lots more and help the Royal Society for the Protection of Birds ensure that there will still be as many, in fact more, visiting your garden in a hundred years from now.

◀HOOPOE ▲WAXWING

UNUSUAL BIRDS

Here are two not often seen, but unmistakable when they are. You may be lucky enough to spy a **Hoopoe** probing for insects on a lawn in spring, or a **Waxwing** in winter. Waxwings are seen in large numbers every few years, but usually just small parties feeding on berried shrubs in the Eastern Counties.

Tell me what unusual bird you saw, and when and where, please! ....Score **50**

The YOUNG ORNITHOLOGISTS' CLUB is for all boys and girls interested in birds. For details of the club or for a free leaflet on how to make a bird table, write to Y.O.C., The Lodge, Sandy, Bedfordshire.

The address of the WILDFOWL TRUST is:-
Slimbridge, Near Gloucester, Glos. GL2 7BT

JOIN THE I-SPY CLUB

- All you need to join the I-SPY Club is to buy a Membership Book which includes the secret codes. Ask at your bookshop or newsagent.

- Tell your friends about I-SPY. Invite them to join and form a Patrol with you.

- Collect all the I-SPY books – and you'll have a wonderful library of your own.

- Write to me about any interesting discoveries you make. You may win a prize! Remember to enclose a stamped addressed envelope for a reply.

LOOK OUT FOR THESE I-SPY WITH DAVID BELLAMY BOOKS

AT THE AIRPORT	GARDEN FLOWERS
ARCHAEOLOGY	ALL THE YEAR
AT THE ART	ROUND
GALLERY	GARDEN BIRDS
BIRDS AND	MAMMALS AT THE
REPTILES AT	ZOO
THE ZOO	NIGHT SKY
BRITISH COINS	ON A DAY AT THE
BRITISH WILDLIFE	SEASIDE
CREEPY CRAWLIES	ON A FARM
ON A CAR	ON A TRAIN
JOURNEY	JOURNEY
CAR NUMBERS	PETS
CARS	POND LIFE
CIVIL AIRCRAFT	SUPERMARKETS
DINOSAURS	TREES
FISH AND FISHING	WILD FLOWERS

AND MANY MORE TO COME

INDEX

ACKNOWLEDGEMENTS

Illustrations by Anthony Maynard. 'Shell Times' for David Bellamy's photograph on page 2. Series Editor Anthony Maynard.

Published by Ravette Limited, 12 Star Road, Partridge Green, Horsham, West Sussex RH13 8RA   Ravette Ltd. 1983. Printed in Italy (KEL)
ISBN 0-906710-30-8